KOREANS

in America

KOREANS

in America

Wayne Patterson
Hyung-chan Kim

 Lerner Publications Company • Minneapolis

Page 2: A Korean family in Hawaii, about 1920

1992 REVISED EDITION

Library of Congress Cataloging-in-Publication Data

Patterson, Wayne, 1946-
   Koreans in America / Wayne Patterson, Hyung-Chan
Kim. — Rev. ed.
      p.   cm. — (The In America series)
   Includes index.
   Summary: Surveys the immigration of Koreans to
America from 1903 to the present time and identifies the
contributions of individual Koreans to American life and
culture.
   ISBN 0-8225-0248-8 (lib. bdg.)
   ISBN 0-8225-1045-6 (pbk.)
   1. Korean Americans—History—Juvenile literature.
[1. Korean Americans.] I. Kim, Hyung-Chan. II. Title.
III. Series.
   E184.K6P37   1992
   973'.04957—dc20   91-46494
                                                CIP
                                                 AC

Manufactured in the United States of America

4   5   6   7   8   9   97   96   95   94   93   92

CONTENTS

1
CENTURIES OF CONFLICT

The Lee family, of Wilmette, Illinois, emigrated from Inchon, South Korea, in 1976.

A Growing Population

Throughout most of its long history, the small country of Korea has been surrounded and dominated by three powerful nations—Japan, China, and Russia. From time to time, Korea has also limited its contacts with Western countries. In fact, until fairly recently—when the Korean War of the 1950s put Korea in the world spotlight—people in the West knew little about the country and its people.

Years before the Korean War, however, Koreans had learned about the Western lands. Thousands of Koreans began to leave their homeland for the West during the 19th century. And in the early 20th century, Koreans began to go to the United States.

For several decades, the Korean-American population was very small, never numbering above a few thousand. But in the mid-1960s, the U.S. government eased its restrictions on Asian immigration, and the number of Korean Americans increased by tens of thousands every year. There were 70,000 Korean Americans in 1970 and 350,000 in 1980. By 1990 Korean Americans numbered nearly 800,000. Most Korean Americans live in large urban areas, and more live in Los Angeles than in any other city in the nation.

For many of these immigrants, the move to the United States has been difficult. Korean Americans have not always been welcomed in their new country. They have faced discriminatory laws from the courts, and they have become involved in bitter race wars on city streets. But the Korean-American community is strong. Korean Americans are surviving and thriving, and they are making valuable contributions to America's landscape and culture.

In the mid-1960s, the U.S. government eased its restrictions on Asian immigration, and the number of Korean Americans increased by tens of thousands every year.

China and the Three Kingdoms

When we speak of present-day Korea, we are actually talking about two countries—the Republic of Korea, or South Korea, and the Democratic People's Republic of Korea, also called North Korea. Both nations share a small East Asian peninsula that divides the Yellow Sea and the East Sea (also called the Sea of Japan). But these two countries have existed separately for just a short time. For thousands of years, the peninsula was one nation, which people in the West came to know as Korea.

Korean legend says that the country was founded in 2333 B.C., by a priest named Tangun—the son of a heavenly prince and a bear that had been transformed into a woman. Tangun named his kingdom Choson, and it existed for more than 1,000 years.

In the third century B.C., China invaded Choson. Although China eventually lost all its authority over

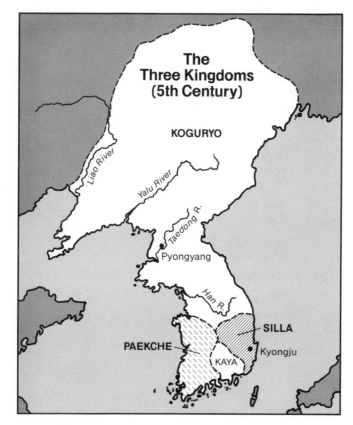

The Three Kingdoms (5th Century)

KOGURYO

Liao River

Yalu River

Taedong R.

Pyongyang

Han R.

PAEKCHE

KAYA

SILLA

Kyongju

For centuries Korea's three kingdoms fought for control of the peninsula. This map shows the fifth-century boundaries of Koguryo, Silla, and Paekche.

the smaller country, the Chinese retained a strong cultural influence over Korea for more than 400 years. The religion of Buddhism came to Korea by way of China, as did Confucianism, a philosophy that would eventually become one of the strongest forces in Korean ideas, values, and behavior.

During the second and third centuries A.D., the people of the Korean peninsula established three powerful kingdoms—Koguryo, Paekche, and Silla. Near the end of the seventh century, Silla conquered the two neighboring kingdoms and united the Korean peninsula under a single ruling family, or dynasty. By the mid-eighth century, Silla's power had reached its peak. Although a handful of wealthy people lived comfortable lives, many more Korean people lived as slaves. Power struggles broke out among many of the wealthy families. By 900, Korean leaders had split Silla apart and reestablished the three kingdoms of Silla, Koguryo, and Paekche.

Over the next few decades, the three kingdoms fought for rule over the entire peninsula. In A.D. 936, the Koguryo kingdom conquered the peninsula, and Koguryo's leader, Wang Kon, named the region Koryo. (The modern name Korea is derived from the name of this region.) The Koryo kingdom prospered for four centuries of Korea's history, leaving behind a rich legacy of artistic, scientific, and literary achievement. Building on China's advances in printing, for example, Koreans invented the world's first movable printing type in 1234.

The strength of the Koryo kingdom did not last, however. Forces from Mongolia, north of Korea, invaded Koryo in 1231 and conquered the kingdom. Mongols dominated Koryo until 1368, when the Chinese Ming dynasty pushed the Mongols back to the north.

Koreans made many advances in printing and publication. These wooden printing blocks for Buddhist scriptures were carved in the 13th century.

The complete fall of Koryo finally came in 1392. Some of Koryo's leaders wanted to maintain ties with the Mongols, while other leaders wanted to develop ties with the Ming. The king of Koryo ordered a Koryo military commander, General Yi Song-gye, to attack Ming forces. But General Yi revolted. He turned his army against Koryo's capital and seized the throne. Yi founded the Choson dynasty (sometimes called the Yi dynasty), which lasted until the early 20th century.

It was during the Choson dynasty that Buddhism began to be viewed as corrupt, and Confucianism became popular with both government officials and the common people of Korea. Confucianism is not a religion like Buddhism. It is a philosophy of life and a system of ethics. Confucianism describes relationships between rulers and subjects, parents and children, husbands and wives, and the young and the old. It teaches the people to obey their rulers, and it teaches the rulers to govern their people with wisdom, goodwill, and kindness.

The Hermit Kingdom

The first two hundred years of the Choson period were generally peaceful. Then, in the 16th century, foreign invasions began. Korea was attacked by the Japanese in 1592 and 1597, and again by a people called the Manchus (a group that went on to conquer China and establish a dynasty there) in 1627 and 1636. With help from the Chinese army, the Koreans were able to drive away the Japanese. But they could not drive away the Manchu armies. Although the Choson dynasty survived, these attacks destroyed much of Korea's land and many villages.

Throughout the 16th and 17th centuries, certain Korean scholars began rejecting Confucianism. The scholars took a new interest in Western science, technology, and religion, which were coming to Choson by way of China. These Western influences

The writings of Chinese philosopher Confucius describe ethical behavior and respect for authority.

worried the traditional Korean rulers, who saw change and new ideas as a threat to their power. In addition, Korean merchants were beginning to engage in trade with foreign lands. The merchant class grew wealthier and more influential. To keep the merchant class from becoming too powerful, ruling landowners discouraged international trade and commerce. They tried to suppress all Korean contact with outsiders.

Despite the rulers' attempts to suppress Western influences, modern weapons, gunpowder, maps, and telescopes came to Korea through China. Western books—and with them, Western thought—also slipped into the country. Even Catholicism made its way to Korea, also through the Chinese, who had received visits from Portuguese missionaries. The Christian faith appealed to Koreans because it taught that equality and eternal salvation were the rights of everyone. But this new religion also conflicted with the traditional Confucian social order, and in the late 1700s Choson officials outlawed Christian missionaries and the practice of Catholicism.

This Christian monastery was established in Korea by a group of German missionaries.

11

Korea and the West

Prior to the 19th century, China and Japan also isolated themselves from the rest of the world. But in doing so, these nations failed to keep pace with Western military technology. By the 1830s, both China and Japan were feeling threatened by Western powers. And a series of military defeats over the next several decades caused China, Japan, and finally Korea to cooperate and trade with Western nations.

Boats from foreign lands appeared at Korean ports, carrying not only Western products but also people from Western lands. New railroads linked the capital in Seoul with other important cities in Korea. With the completion of the Trans-Siberian Railway across Asia, it became possible to travel from Korea to Europe in less than a week. Koreans also began to travel to Japan and the United States, and many of them returned with new ideas about government and technology.

Amid these developments, Korea's rulers also repealed the laws that forbade Christian missionaries to enter the country. American Protestants and Catholics entered Korea, and they brought their political as well as their religious views with them. Missionaries established schools, and students at American-founded schools grew more interested in seeing a democratic political system established in Korea.

In the 1890s, Koreans began publishing daily newspapers. The first paper, called *The Independent,* was established by a Korean named Philip Jaisohn, who had studied in the United States and had returned to help his country adopt the more modern ways of the West. Soon other newspapers sprang up, publishing stories about the people and customs of faraway lands. For the first time, average Korean citizens began to think about the world that lay beyond their own little villages. Suddenly it was possible to read about—and perhaps even to visit—these strange new lands.

Philip Jaisohn was the first Korean to become a U.S. citizen and the first Korean-American doctor.

Korea and Japan

Following the Russo-Japanese War, Japan gained control of Choson.

Many Koreans thought that Western ideas brought improvements. But as foreign influences in Korea expanded, the political situation in the country grew violent. In 1894 followers of the *Tonghak* ("Eastern learning") movement rebelled against the nation's government. The king of Choson asked Chinese troops to help fight the rebels, and when the Japanese sent in their own forces, the conflict erupted into the Chinese-Japanese War. In 1895 Japan defeated China and the Tonghak rebels.

The wars and rebellions of the 1890s left many Koreans homeless. People were forced to leave their farms in the countryside and head for the cities or seaports in search of what little work was available there. And in addition to these hardships, corrupt government officials taxed the people so heavily that many citizens went into debt just to survive.

At the same time, Russia also began to increase its influence in Choson. Russia first took over parts of northeastern China, then claimed a large portion of Choson's forests and mines. The question of who would control Choson—Japan or Russia—caused a conflict that eventually erupted in the Russo-Japanese War. In 1905 Japan defeated Russia, establishing itself as a major world power. Japan made Choson a "protectorate," meaning that the nation was under Japan's protection and control. In 1910 Japan annexed Choson.

Under Japanese rule, life for the Koreans became much worse than before. Over the next several decades, the Japanese government attempted to wipe out Korean culture. Japan took half the country's rice crop and forced Koreans off their land. By 1910 Japan had taken control of every Korean school and temple. By the 1930s, Japanese leaders had ordered Koreans to worship at shrines of Shintoism (the Japanese religion), to speak the Japanese language in schools, and to adopt Japanese names. The Japanese leaders also prevented Koreans from publishing their own newspapers and from organizing political or intellectual groups.

This bronze mural, displayed in Seoul's Pagoda Park, honors the Koreans who demonstrated against Japanese rule.

In response to this oppression, thousands of Koreans participated in demonstrations—most of them peaceful marches. But some protests erupted into riots, and over time Japanese soldiers killed a total of 7,000 Koreans and imprisoned 50,000 more. Entire villages were destroyed, and the country fell into almost complete ruin.

Those who were lucky escaped the country. Some Koreans fled to nearby China or Russia, and a few went to the United States.

A refugee family approaches the border between the north and south parts of Korea after World War II.

A Divided Country

With the United States' declaration of war against Japan in 1941, Koreans renewed their hopes. They believed that if Japan were defeated, Korea would be free again. But with the outbreak of World War II, living conditions in Korea actually worsened. Food became scarce, and Japanese oppression increased. Even Japan's defeat by the United States in 1945 did

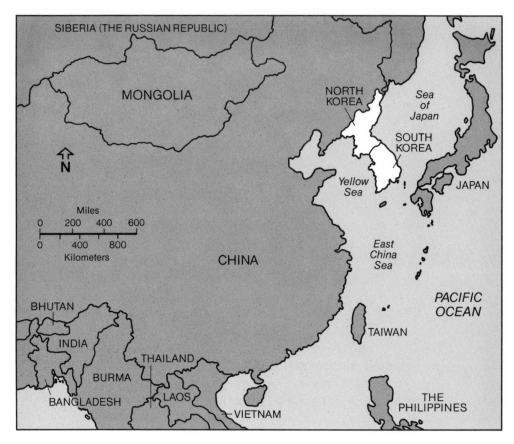

not bring the new era of freedom that the Koreans had hoped for.

Since 1948 Korea has been a divided country.

At the war's end, Japan was required to give up all the territory it had acquired after 1894. This territory included Korea. The United States and the Soviet Union divided the Korean peninsula at the 38th degree of north latitude. Soviet troops occupied the northern section, and U.S. troops remained in the south.

Both powers considered this division to be temporary, and the United States and the Soviet Union worked for the next two years to reunify Korea. Negotiations between the two countries broke down, however, and the United States submitted the problem of reunification to the United Nations. The United Nations offered to supervise elections in Korea so

Syngman Rhee

the people could choose one government, but the Soviet Union refused to let the UN representatives hold elections in the north.

People in the south held elections in 1948, choosing a national assembly that then drew up a constitution. In July 1948, Syngman Rhee won the presidential election, and a month later the south formed the Republic of Korea. Later that year, the north announced the formation of the Democratic People's Republic of Korea, under Communist leader Kim Il Sung.

In June 1950, war broke out between the two parts of the divided country. North Korean armies invaded South Korean territory, capturing the capital city of Seoul within three days. When the United Nations demanded that the armies withdraw from the region, North Korea ignored the order. Two days after the invasion, the United Nations sent U.S. troops in to help the South Koreans. But when the American forces began to penetrate territory near the Chinese border, China entered the war on the side of the North Koreans.

The war continued for three years, from 1950 to 1953, ending finally in a cease-fire agreement. But, although the fighting stopped, Korea remained divided, controlled by two separate governments.

South Korean university students try to break through riot police lines in anti-government demonstrations (above and left).

A 2.5-mile-wide (4-kilometer-wide) buffer area called the Demilitarized Zone (DMZ) still divides the two sides.

Modern Government

South Korean voters reelected President Syngman Rhee in 1952 and in 1956. After he won the presidency again in 1960 — in an unopposed election — student protesters successfully pressured him to resign.

In May 1961, General Park Chung-hee led a military overthrow and took control of the South Korean government. He then called for elections, and voters elected him president in 1963. Then, in both 1967 and 1971, Park won reelection by a wide margin. He altered the constitution to increase his power and to allow himself to serve an unlimited number of terms. He also changed the presidential election process from direct voting by the people to an electoral system dominated by his own supporters. Park was reelected by the electoral college in 1972 and again in 1978. He began to limit freedoms of speech, of the press, and of assembly, and he jailed his opponents. General Park's tyranny seemed unstoppable. Then, in 1979, Park was assassinated by Kim Jae-gyu, the director of the Korean Central Intelligence Agency.

Although a military government ruled South Korea through most of the 1980s, political freedom in South Korea eventually increased. Direct elections are being held once again. But the country is still not at peace. Citizens demanding reunification often stage protests, and violent student riots are frequent sights on the streets of Seoul. In the quieter nation of North Korea, Kim Il Sung has led his country continuously since the Communist government was established in 1948. But as long as political boundaries separate families and friends, neither North Koreans nor South Koreans will be satisfied with the state of their nation. Citizens on both sides of the DMZ look forward to a time when their divided country will again be whole.

Direct elections are being held once again. But the country is still not at peace.

2
IMMIGRANTS TO AMERICA

Plantation Workers

The Hawaiian islands have drawn laborers and immigrants from Asia for many years. In the mid-1800s, the expansion of Hawaii's sugar industry prompted many Asian people to look to the Hawaiian sugar plantations for work. At first most laborers came from China and Japan, but the American growers later tried to recruit workers from Korea as well.

Horace Allen

Although Hawaii was not yet a part of the United States, the plantation owners hoped that the United States would annex the islands. If Hawaii were made a U.S. territory, growers could sell Hawaiian sugar in the United States tax-free. But anti-Chinese feelings were strong in the United States at the time. If they brought over too many Chinese workers, the growers reasoned, the United States might be less inclined to annex Hawaii.

The planters also knew that annexation would bring Hawaii under the laws of the United States. Because of America's Chinese Exclusion Act—an 1882 law that prohibited immigration of Chinese people to the United States—Chinese workers would no longer be allowed to enter Hawaii. The new laws also meant that Asian workers would be protected by certain U.S. labor laws. Labor strikes would become legal on the Hawaiian plantations, and the sugar growers feared an increase in worker protests. So in 1896 the government of Hawaii passed a law requiring that 10 percent of new plantation laborers be from places other than China or Japan.

In 1900, when the Hawaiian islands became an official U.S. territory, plantation workers did go on

Part of a Korean village on a Hawaiian sugar plantation

strike in large numbers. Many other Chinese and Japanese workers–citing severe discrimination and exploitation–simply quit their jobs and left the islands. They returned to their homelands or moved to the U.S. mainland, especially to California. The labor situation for the Hawaiian sugar industry was at its worst.

At about this time, the plantation owners began to hear favorable reports about Korean workers. In 1902 the growers sent a representative to San Francisco to meet with Horace Allen, the American ambassador to Korea. Allen said that Korean workers had done well in Japan and Russia, and that they wanted to leave Korea. The Koreans were suffering under government oppression, he explained. To make matters worse, a severe drought had hit Korea earlier that year, causing starvation among many of the nation's poor.

On his return to Korea, Allen eagerly began recruiting workers for the plantations. He sought the help of a young man named David William Deshler. Deshler owned a steamship service that operated between Korea and Japan. He could easily arrange for the transportation of Korean workers to Japan and then to Hawaii. The Hawaiian Sugar Planters Association (HSPA) paid David Deshler $55 for every Korean recruited to work in Hawaii.

Though the transportation was not a problem, Allen and Deshler had other difficulties to work out. First, Ambassador Allen had to assure the Korean ruler, Kojong, that Korea's government would benefit politically and financially from the plan. A government bureau of emigration had to be set up to issue the necessary passports. And David Deshler needed to open his own bank—the "Deshler Bank"—which he set up in the Korean city of Inchon. Although a U.S. immigration law prevented employers from giving direct financial assistance to foreign workers coming to the United States, the HSPA got around the law by financing the Korean workers indirectly through the Deshler bank. All the bank's money came from the HSPA, and these funds were lent to Koreans who wanted to work in Hawaii. Without this aid, most of the workers would have been unable to afford the trip.

Some Asian workers were employed in company stores on the sugar plantations. Their jobs were easier than the backbreaking work of the field hands.

Finally, Deshler's agents began to advertise the available jobs. The agents distributed posters that described the advantages of working on the islands:

The climate is suitable for everyone and there is no severe heat or cold. There are schools on every island. English is taught and the tuition is free. There are jobs available all year long for farmers who are healthy and decent in behavior. The monthly pay is $15. The work day is 10 hours long and Sunday is free. Housing, fuel, water, and hospital expenses will be paid by the employer.

Despite the attractive offer, it was not easy to convince Korean workers to leave their homes. Workers had left Korea before, but travel to Hawaii was very different from any journey to Russia or Japan. These countries were relatively close to Korea, and the workers had felt that they could easily return home whenever they wanted. But Hawaii was more than halfway across the Pacific Ocean, and people feared that if they went to Hawaii they could never return home.

A Korean plantation worker

In the end, the task of recruiting workers for the Hawaiian sugar plantations was accomplished through the efforts of American Christian missionaries in Korea. Convincing their Korean converts that they would become better Christians in a Christian country, the missionaries urged Koreans to make the move. David Deshler got his recruits.

On December 22, 1902, the first group of Korean workers—about 120 men and women—left their homeland. They arrived in Hawaii on January 13, 1903—the first of 65 shiploads of Koreans who would make the long journey across the Pacific. But nearly three years later, the migration came to an abrupt end.

In January 1905, another emigration company persuaded about 1,000 Koreans to go to Mexico as laborers. A few months later, a Korean merchant discovered that the laborers were working under slavelike conditions and he immediately notified the Korean government. After hearing about the plight of the Koreans in Mexico, the government prohibited all Korean immigration to both Mexico and Hawaii.

It was later that year that Korea became Japan's protectorate, and, in 1908, the Japanese and U.S. governments issued a law called the Gentlemen's Agreement that virtually stopped all Korean emigration. According to the law, emigration was prohibited for both Japanese and Korean laborers.

The ambitious program to bring Korean laborers to work in the sugarcane fields came to an end. But between 1903 and 1905, roughly 7,000 Koreans came to Hawaii. Of this number, 5,000 would remain in the United States for the rest of their lives.

Moving to the Mainland

Like the Chinese and Japanese before them, many of the Koreans who came to Hawaii did not intend to stay permanently on the islands. The Korean workers only intended to stay for a short time, make some money, and then return home to Korea. But when Japan annexed Korea in 1910, many Koreans decided to stay in Hawaii until their country was free and independent once again. Other Koreans simply could not afford to return to their homeland. Because of the low wages on the plantations and the high cost of living in Hawaii, they had difficulty saving enough money for the boat passage back to Korea. As a result, only about 2,000 Korean laborers eventually returned home.

Of those who remained in Hawaii, few wanted to stay on the plantations. Plantation work was hard, and it was unrewarding. The laborers worked 10-hour days, six days a week, in the hot sun. The barracks they lived in were often overcrowded. When they first arrived in Hawaii, the Koreans stayed on the plantations because they felt they had no choice. But as they became more familiar with American

A boarding school student in Honolulu, about 1910

ways and customs, most Koreans decided that they would be better off if they found other jobs.

Most of the Korean immigrants decided to stay in Hawaii and look for work in the cities, especially in Honolulu. There some of them found jobs in seaports or at pineapple canneries. But anti-Asian discrimination existed even in Hawaii, and whites often refused to hire Asians for some of the better jobs. As a result, many Koreans were forced to fall back on their own resources. They set up small businesses, and Koreans soon became successful in shoe repair, clothing alteration, furniture sales, laundry, and grocery businesses.

Other Koreans who left the plantations decided to try their luck on the U.S. mainland. Eventually, about 1,000 of the Korean plantation workers went to California, Oregon, and Washington, where they found jobs on railroads or as migrant farm workers. Several hundred others traveled to Montana, Utah, Wyoming, and Colorado to work in copper and coal mines.

Many Asian immigrants to Honolulu found work at Dole's pineapple canneries.

25

Some even made their way to Alaska, where they found work in the fish canneries. Wherever they went, Koreans were particularly successful in establishing their own businesses.

Junior Police Officers in Hawaii, about 1926

Over the years, many Koreans ended up in Los Angeles, California. By the 1940s, in Los Angeles alone, Korean immigrants owned more than 30 fruit and vegetable stands, 9 groceries, 8 laundries, 6 trucking companies, 5 wholesale establishments, 5 restaurants, and 3 drugstores. Koreans had begun to make their mark in the United States.

Picture Brides

Of the original 7,000 Koreans in Hawaii, only about 700 were women. And the virtual ban on emigration from Korea in 1908 meant that no more Korean women were expected to come. Under the Gentlemen's Agreement, only students and the wives, children, and parents of those already in the United States were allowed to immigrate.

Because of this imbalance between the numbers of Korean men and women, Korean men often used what was called the "picture-bride" system. Also used by the Japanese and the Chinese, this unusual method of courtship brought many Asian women to America between 1910 and 1924.

A Korean man would have his picture taken and sent to his family in Korea. In return, the man's relatives or a matchmaker hired by his family would send him a picture of a marriageable Korean woman. If the man and the woman decided they wanted to marry each other, the man would send his prospective bride about $100 for traveling expenses. When the young woman arrived in Hawaii, the couple would be married right on the docks. That way the woman could legally enter the United States as the wife of an existing immigrant.

Not all the picture-bride marriages turned out well. When the picture brides arrived in Hawaii and first met their intended husbands, they discovered

The graduating class of a Korean language school in Hawaii

A Korean war bride, with her mother-in-law, at home in Pennsylvania

that the men were poor and that they were older than they looked in their photographs. In fact, some of these husbands were so old that they soon died, leaving the picture brides widowed. Other marriages ended in divorce. Despite the high rate of failure, about 1,000 Korean women entered the United States in this way.

The Korean War

Between 1924 and 1951, the only Koreans to enter the United States were a few hundred political refugees who had managed to slip out of Korea illegally. But the stationing of American troops in Korea during the Korean War increased contact between the two countries that would eventually open new doors for Korean immigration.

More than 5 million American troops served in the course of the three-year Korean War, and less than 1 percent of these soldiers were women. Many of the male soldiers met and married Korean women, and when the soldiers were sent back to the United States, they took their new wives with them. These "war brides" were the first Korean immigrants legally allowed into the United States after 1924.

When the Korean War ended, the United States and South Korea signed a treaty that allowed the United States to station American soldiers in South Korea. Bases and airports were built, and about 50,000 American soldiers remained in the country after 1953. Marriages between American soldiers and Korean women continued for many years following the war. Between 1951 and 1964, more than 28,000 Korean war brides immigrated to the United States.

Another large group immigrating to the United States at this time were Korean children. Many had been orphaned by the war. Others were fathered by American soldiers who left the country at the war's end. Because Confucian tradition does not easily

For several decades, Americans have adopted children from Korean orphanages.

accept fatherless children or children of mixed ethnic backgrounds, many single Korean mothers chose to give up their children for adoption. The children could not have happy lives in Korea, their mothers felt. American charitable societies and Christian adoption agencies found adoptive parents for these children in the United States.

Although peace was established in Korea in 1953, tensions remained high in the country for many years. The war had left Korea almost completely ruined. Its economy was wrecked, and the Korean people were on the brink of poverty and starvation. In addition, South Korea lost most of its democratic freedoms under Syngman Rhee and Park Chung-hee. Many Korean intellectuals wanted to come to the United States, which held the promise of freedom and democracy and which had no constant threat of war. To the majority of Koreans, the United States sounded like a land of opportunity where a family could have a secure future.

The United States sounded like a land of opportunity where a family could have a secure future.

New Immigration

The Immigration and Naturalization Act of 1952 allowed people of all races and nationalities to immigrate to the United States. This law carried a provision, however, that the number of immigrants from each country would be restricted by a certain quota. Just a small fraction of the Koreans who wanted to immigrate were allowed into the country.

Thirteen years later, in 1965, the U.S. government finally lifted these quotas. But the government was still selective about who was let in to the United States, favoring applicants who were professionals with needed skills. Doctors, nurses, and scientists were the first to be admitted. Applicants with relatives who were U.S. citizens were also preferred immigrants, and, because many Koreans already lived in the United States, the number of Koreans immigrating each year shot up to about 15,000.

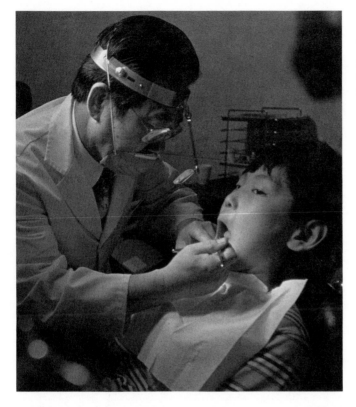

Thousands of Korean medical professionals have immigrated to the United States.

Many of these family members were unskilled workers. Yet so many Korean professionals also left their country that Korea's leaders feared a "brain drain"—that is, a significant loss of scientists, scholars, and other people whose talents were needed at home. The Korean government then put restrictions on the number of people who could leave Korea, and many people were put on waiting lists for years.

Korea has since eased its restrictions on emigration, mostly because of the country's problem of over-population. Family members of U.S. citizens are still the biggest group of Korean immigrants to the United States, while some Koreans leave because of urban overpopulation and economic and political troubles at home. Still others are simply attracted to America's culture. Altogether, about 30,000 immigrants come to the United States from Korea each year. All hope to find a better life in the United States.

3
A KOREAN-AMERICAN COMMUNITY

Professional and Business Success

Of the first Korean immigrants to Hawaii, very few were able to read or write in English. This was a handicap in the United States that prevented Korean immigrants from entering most professions. These immigrants made sure that their children learned English, however. They also encouraged their children to study in U.S. colleges and universities and to earn advanced degrees. As a result, many second-generation Korean Americans were able to enter professions such as teaching, medicine, and law.

The English language is still a barrier for recent Korean immigrants. To enter the U.S. job market in their chosen fields, immigrants must be able to read and write English and pass literacy tests. Many must return to school to study English, and they are still not guaranteed high-paying jobs. A study done in San Francisco in 1980 showed that over a broad range of professions, Korean immigrant men earned only 60 percent of what their white counterparts earned.

But many Korean immigrants are succeeding, despite signs of discrimination, and despite language barriers. For several decades, many Korean Americans have found a niche for themselves in small business. And the number of successful Korean-American businesses is increasing each year. A 1988 survey found that a startling number—52 percent—of Korean Americans in New York City owned their own businesses.

A Korean-American teacher helps a student.

In the late 1960s, Korean immigrants arriving in New York found the neighborhood businesses in transition. The owners of Jewish and Italian family markets—people who had operated most of the city's fruit and vegetable stands for decades—wanted to retire. Their children were pursuing other professions, and the owners needed to sell. Korean immigrants saw valuable opportunities in these "greengroceries," which were for sale at reasonable prices.

Since that time, Korean immigrants in nearly every U.S. city have opened small retail stores of all kinds. They have learned that retail businesses have a rapid cash flow, and that the start-up costs are fairly low. In addition, these small shops can be run by people who do not speak fluent English.

Unfortunately, many Korean Americans are not happy in their businesses. Many would prefer to be working in other fields. One survey taken during the late 1980s found that over 75 percent of New York's Korean greengrocers had college degrees in such diverse fields as engineering, medicine, computers, and nuclear physics. Until more employers will give

Many Korean Americans have found success in retail businesses such as New York City's greengroceries.

33

Asian Americans fair opportunities and equal pay, however, Korean Americans are likely to remain in business for themselves.

Not every Korean American can afford to buy a business, so Korean Americans often help each other make down payments. Using an ancient Korean system of lending money, a group of about 10 people will meet once a month, over a traditional meal at a Korean restaurant. At every monthly meeting, each member contributes a fixed amount of money to a fund called a *kye*. Each month a different member is allowed to take a turn borrowing the sum of the money. When the cycle is complete, each kye member has had a turn borrowing the lump sum and has been able to make a larger investment than he or she would have been able to make alone.

Another source of help for many new business-people is the Korean Produce Association, established in 1974. Through a newsletter and a newspaper, the association exchanges market information, matching new greengrocers with established Korean suppliers, distributors, and contractors. Most Korean greengrocers belong to the association, which has the size and the influence to buy good produce at good prices. Korean merchants often feel that discrimination can slow the process of establishing a new business. But with aid from the Korean Produce Association, a new greengrocer is able to set up a store quickly, sometimes in just a few weeks.

The number of Korean-owned stores in New York City reached its peak in 1990. At that time, the city's Korean-American population owned about 15,500 small businesses. But New York's economy has faltered in recent years, and rising taxes and dropping sales have threatened the stability of the city's Korean businesses. While the troubles can be linked to a nationwide recession, they are also at least partly due to the Korean Americans' past success. Korean-American merchants have competed with one another for a limited market, and they have driven up their own rents.

Most Korean Americans live in large cities such as San Francisco, New York, Chicago, Los Angeles, Honolulu, and Washington, D.C. Many of these cities have large Korean-American neighborhoods, known as "Koreatowns."

The Korean Produce Association has asked its members to stop competing directly with each other, but with little success. New Korean immigrants have begun to avoid New York and are opening businesses in more promising locations in the South, the West, and the Southwest. Other Korean Americans are staying away from inner cities and moving to the suburbs.

If Korean Americans do leave their urban neighborhoods, they can be proud of the legacy they have left behind. Koreans have revitalized many of these neighborhoods. In the 1960s, the area that now is home to Los Angeles' Korean community was considered a slum. But with the start-up of Korean-owned businesses, property values in this area grew to at least 20 times their mid-1960s levels. And the thousands of small, Korean-owned shops around the country have contributed billions of dollars to the U.S. economy.

The Japanese bombing of Pearl Harbor Naval Base in Hawaii increased many people's resentment against Asian Americans.

Facing Prejudice

Anti-Asian prejudice in the United States existed before many Americans had ever heard of Korea. Its beginnings go back to a period of Chinese immigration in the mid-1800s. Prejudice against Japanese Americans also preceded most Korean immigrants to the United States. In fact, it is only fairly recently that Korean Americans have become a specific target of prejudice. Through the first part of the 20th century, the Korean-American population was not large enough to be noticed by most other Americans. The Korean Americans were a minority within a minority, often lumped together with other Asians. But in this way, Korean Americans have been caught up in the general tide of anti-Asian sentiment.

In 1906 a San Francisco judge ruled that Asian students couldn't attend public schools in white districts. A 1913 U.S. law made it illegal for Asians to own property. The Oriental Exclusion Act of 1924 banned all Asian immigration to the United States for nearly 40 years. Asians have been barred from American restaurants, hotels, and public swimming pools. During the unemployment and poverty of the economic depression following World War I, prejudice against all Asians worsened. Whites sometimes accused Asian immigrants of taking "their" jobs. During World War II, anti-Asian sentiment soared, and Japanese Americans were evacuated from their homes and placed in internment camps.

Because Koreans in America were enthusiastic supporters of the war against Japan, many volunteered to fight in Asia. And because they could speak, read, and write Japanese, some Korean Americans were used as language teachers and translators by the U.S. Army. About 100 Koreans in Los Angeles joined the California Home Guard, while others served in the Red Cross. Korean-American organizations bought war bonds, and individuals wrote to their local newspapers to express their support of the U.S. troops.

In spite of all this, the war years were particularly difficult for Koreans in America. Since Korea was officially part of the Japanese empire, the American government was not sure how to treat Koreans. They were not sent to relocation camps like the Japanese Americans, but they were not treated fairly, either. In Hawaii, for example, Koreans were labeled "enemy aliens" for a time and were not allowed to work at military bases.

The Korean-American population has grown much more visible in recent years, and a different kind of prejudice has emerged. In 1985, shoppers in Chicago's South Side picketed many Korean-owned stores, complaining that the stores would not accept returned merchandise. Between 1984 and 1986, 11 Korean-owned shops in a single Washington, D.C., neighborhood were firebombed. In the summer of 1986, Koreans in a Philadelphia neighborhood battled with their neighbors over Korean-language street signs. After the Korean residents had won the city's permission to put up the signs, vandals bent or tore down the signs or draped them with American flags. The city ordered the signs removed within months.

The war years were particularly difficult for Koreans in America. Since Korea was officially part of the Japanese empire, the American government was not sure how to treat Korean Americans.

A heavily publicized race war started in January 1990 in the Flatbush section of Brooklyn, New York. There, a Haitian immigrant accused a Korean immigrant—a fruit and vegetable market employee—of assaulting her during an argument. The incident prompted blacks to boycott two Korean stores, in a neighborhood where racial tensions had already started to boil. And during the April 1992 rioting in South Central Los Angeles, black rioters targeted Korean businesses in the area.

Relations between Korean and black inner-city communities have been strained for years. In both Los Angeles and New York, black shoppers commonly complain that Korean merchants treat them rudely and refuse to extend them credit or hire black employees.

At least part of this conflict can be attributed to cultural differences. In the Korean culture, strangers do not usually smile at one another, and direct eye contact is considered aggressive. Women are taught not to touch strangers. In the United States, where

Violence followed the boycotts of Korean-American groceries in Brooklyn.

A man defies the boycott of a Brooklyn grocery store.

smiling, direct eye contact, and touch are signs of friendliness, the behavior of the Korean-American shopkeepers can be misinterpreted as rudeness.

Another source of prejudice against Korean Americans is the rumor that the U.S. government helps Korean immigrants get their start in business. Only political refugees are entitled to money from the U.S. government, however, and almost all South Koreans are non-political refugees. Still another rumor is that Korean grocers receive financing from Reverend Sun Myung Moon, the Korean evangelist who founded the Unification Church.

The real advantages that many Korean immigrants have are their high levels of education, and the resources available to them because of their strong communities and the tradition of the kye.

Although many of these racial conflicts are far from over, leaders from both the Korean and the black communities have been working together in an effort to end the misunderstandings and the violence. Korean Americans in Los Angeles have held workshops to discuss cultural differences between the two groups. In Philadelphia, Korean merchants have hired dozens of black teenagers to demonstrate the good intentions of the Korean-American community.

Two Different Worlds

Through working in retail businesses, thousands of Korean Americans have found that their hard work can pay off. But for many of them, success comes at a high price. Studies have shown that the Korean-American population suffers from divorce rates and rates of juvenile delinquency that far exceed the national average. Large urban Korean communities, sometimes called "Koreatowns," often have high unemployment rates and high crime rates. Domestic violence is on the rise among Korean-American families, and alcoholism and loneliness are also growing problems in many communities. Experts say that these problems are considered uncommon in the Koreans' home country.

Among Korean business owners, many psychological and social problems can be attributed in part to the exhausting work that they do. Many merchants have found that for their stores to make a profit, they need to stay open as long as 16 to 24 hours per day. The high tensions in some racially mixed neighborhoods add to the stress that the shopkeepers feel. And a great number of Korean Americans encounter overwhelming difficulties as they try to reconcile the differences between life in the United States and the life in Korea that they have left behind.

Korean Americans are often strongly influenced by Confucian tradition, which defines their behavior. They feel they must honor and respect their elders, for example. The American idea of striking out alone in search of success puzzles Korean immigrants, many of whom live in multigenerational homes. But these extended family arrangements can be trying as well. Eventually, many Korean Americans find their homes divided by language barriers, as children

Korean Americans encounter difficulties as they try to reconcile the differences between life in the United States and the life in Korea that they have left behind.

grow up learning English and parents and grand-parents speak Korean.

Another Korean tradition dictates that the head of the household (the father) decides his child's course of study and choice of college, profession, and spouse. Arranged marriages are still preferred in Korean culture. While many young Korean Americans see an arranged marriage as the "right" way, many others do not. This break with tradition has been a source of conflict within a number of Korean-American families.

Korean-American women face special problems, as they try to reconcile the traditional role of wife with that of an American working woman. In Korea married women rarely work outside their homes. But in the United States, nearly two-thirds of Korean-American wives hold jobs. Korean-American women usually work long hours in the family businesses or in garment factories. In addition, these women feel that they must be the sole caretakers of their children and their homes, as Confucian tradition dictates. As

Korean-American women often work in family businesses.

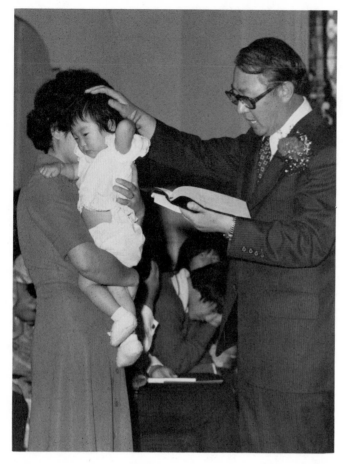

The Christian church and the family are at the center of many Korean-American communities.

a result, Korean-American women are often tremendously overworked. And often both parents in a family feel anxious when their long work hours do not permit them to spend time with their children.

Organizations That Make a Difference

Almost as soon as the first Korean laborers arrived in Hawaii, they began setting up community organizations. One that remains strong is the Korean Christian church.

By 1918 Koreans in Hawaii had established approximately 40 Protestant churches. Nearly 40 percent (about 2,800) of the Korean plantation workers had converted to Christianity. Besides ministering to their congregations, these churches functioned as community centers and schools, offering lessons to members in reading, history, and geography.

Since this time, churches have expanded their role in Korean-American communities. Churches have set up counseling services, in which ministers help newcomers find their way in American society. The churches have also become a prime place for business contacts. And churches are a place where members can speak their native language and keep children in touch with their cultural heritage.

Some Korean Americans say they have converted to Christianity precisely because the church provides these social functions. Although the majority of South Koreans are still Buddhist, even most Buddhist immigrants become Christian when they reach the United States.

Other community centers—including the YMCA and the YWCA—have provided Korean Americans with similar services, such as classes and counseling groups. Korean Americans have also opened youth

Children learn about Korean culture in weekend schools.

centers to battle drug abuse, gang activity, auto theft, and truancy among Korean-American teenagers. New York's Koreatown has nearly 400 weekend Korean schools, where children take classes in Korean history, music, language, cooking, and dance.

To bridge the physical distance between their communities, Korean Americans depend on the growing Korean-American media. In recent years, Korean-language broadcasting has come to southern California's airwaves. There, television and radio stations regularly broadcast Korean music, radio dramas, news shows, and English lessons. Other programs help immigrants adapt to their new culture, with lessons in American life. A particular show may focus on how to rent an apartment, for example, or how to make a flight reservation with an airline. Some stations broadcast news from Korea, and at least two radio stations broadcast Los Angeles Dodger games with Korean commentary.

Cities with large Korean populations may have Korean-American newspapers. Two papers published in Korea also put out American editions in Los Angeles, New York City, and Chicago. For many Korean Americans, these papers provide the most valuable link to their homeland.

Programs help immigrants adapt to their new culture, with lessons in American life.

Return to Korea

Increased tourism between South Korea and the United States is another way that the two countries are becoming closer. Most Korean tourists in the United States come to visit family members who have moved to the United States. As the Korean-American population grows, so does the number of Korean tourists. Since 1989, when the South Korean government lifted restrictions on overseas travel, South Koreans have become the fastest-growing group of U.S. tourists from overseas.

Some Korean Americans also travel to Korea to visit, though for those who have grown up in the

United States, a visit to Korea can inspire culture shock. First-time visitors often cannot accept the way that Korean men dominate Korean women. Many also find that their values clash with Korea's hierarchical family structure. They are frustrated by a society in which younger people must cater to their elders' wishes.

Those who were born in Korea, however, accept this way of life. Some Korean immigrants to the United States have even returned to Korea to live, encouraged by South Korea's improved economy and political reforms. But for many, returning to Korea is next to impossible. The cost of living has soared in South Korea, and many middle-class Korean Americans would be poor there.

Wherever they live, people of Korean heritage often feel united by events in Korea. The protests and the violence there cannot be ignored. And while their country is still divided, reunification is on the minds of Koreans around the world.

The editorial office of the Korea-Times *newspaper in Los Angeles*

For the first time ever, Korean Americans sponsored a float in the 99th-annual Tournament of Roses parade. Donations for the float, a celebration of the 1988 Olympic Games in Seoul, came from all over the Los Angeles area and from South Korea.

4
CONTRIBUTIONS TO AMERICAN LIFE

Government and Public Affairs

A number of Korean Americans have been elected to school boards in the United States, but few have served their government at a higher level. Most Korean immigrants, amid their struggles to survive in a new country, have not found time for politics. Because of Korea's history as a dictatorship, many other Korean Americans have not recognized the significance and power of democratic participation. But this attitude is changing gradually, and many Korean Americans have begun to contribute funds to political candidates, especially to those with Korean ties or sympathies.

Alfred H. Song, born in Hawaii, served in the California state legislature for more than 15 years. He graduated from the University of Southern California, where he received a law degree, then he started his political career in the California state assembly in 1962. Four years later, Song won a seat in the California state senate. He was twice reelected to the senate, in 1970 and again in 1974, but in 1978 Senator Song was defeated in the Democratic primary election.

Herbert Y. C. Choy, a federal judge, was born in 1916 in the town of Makaweli, Kauai, and he grew up in Honolulu, Hawaii. He graduated from the University of Hawaii in 1938 and then studied law at Harvard, receiving his law degree in 1941. But Choy's legal

Herbert Y. C. Choy

career was interrupted by military service when the United States declared war against Japan. Choy entered the army in December 1941 and remained on active duty until 1946, when he became a colonel in the army reserve. Choy was then invited to join the Honolulu law firm of Fong and Miho. For the next 25 years, he practiced law in Honolulu, taking time out to serve as Attorney General of the Territory of Hawaii in 1957 and 1958. Then, in May 1971, President Richard M. Nixon appointed Herbert Choy to the United States Court of Appeals, Ninth Circuit, making Judge Choy the first person of Asian ancestry to be appointed to the federal bench.

Business

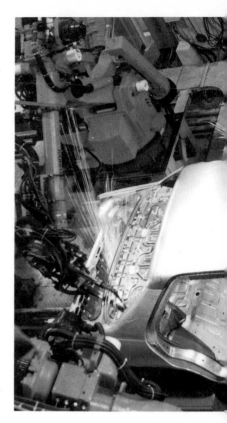

Korean Americans have achieved spectacular success in large businesses as well as in greengroceries and other family-run stores. Andrew Ham is the owner of Olympic Auto Sales & Leasing, an auto dealership in Los Angeles' Koreatown. Cho Hyun Shin, who began working in an auto body shop and then bought a dry cleaning store, is now a multimillionaire real estate broker in New York. Ucho Lee, who came to the United States from South Korea in 1974, first worked as a carpenter in Arlington, Virginia. By 1980 Lee had bought a neighborhood convenience store and by 1987 he had formed Lee's Enterprises, Inc., and was the owner of five businesses and three buildings in Boston.

An early Korean-American entrepreneur, Charles Kim (1884–1968) came to the United States in 1914. With his friend Harry Kim, he founded the Kim Brothers Company in Reedley, California, in 1921. The business started as a small produce and nursery wholesaler. The Kims soon expanded their business, buying orchards, fruit-packing houses, and nurseries, while developing new varieties of fruit trees. Working mainly with nectarines and peaches, they developed the "fuzzless" peaches known as "Le Grand" and "Sun Grand." Both men were active in the Korean

Korea's Hyundai Motor Company now manufactures and sells cars in the United States.

community and helped establish the Korean Community Center in Los Angeles and the Korean Foundation, a fund that awards scholarships to students of Korean ancestry.

Sun Won Sohn is another successful and prominent Korean American. Sohn is chief economist for Norwest Corporation, a bank holding company based in Minneapolis, Minnesota. The company operates in several foreign countries, and Sohn travels to investigate foreign markets and to visit Norwest's overseas customers. Sohn, who came to Norwest Corporation in 1974, was born in Korea.

Community Service

Many Koreans have strong community ties, but several people have made outstanding contributions to their Korean-American communities.

Sonia Suk is a businessperson who has given much of her energy and resources to help Southern California's large Korean-American community. A divorced mother of two children and a cab driver in Korea, Suk immigrated to the United States in 1948 to attend college. She started her first business in the 1950s, making *kimchi*—pickled cabbage—for local markets. With the money she made from the kimchi business, she started a construction firm. Then, in the 1960s, Suk began studying real estate and selling burial plots. She started her own real estate company and began lending money to Koreans for down payments on new businesses.

Sonia Suk

In the 1970s, Suk set up the Korean Town Development Association of Los Angeles, which built most of that city's Koreatown. Through the 1970s and 1980s, Suk helped create almost 40 groups that serve Koreans in southern California. These groups include the Korean Businesswomen's Association, which lends Korean-American women start-up funds for their own small businesses, a senior citizens' association, and a sister city committee that sponsors business exchanges between the United States and Korea. Sonia Suk has also served as president of the Korean Association of Southern California.

Grace Lyu-Volckhausen, following a family tradition of activism, has also donated much time and talent to her community. Back in Korea, Lyu-Volckhausen's mother and grandmother were both active in organizing programs for Korean women. Lyu-Volckhausen was a student activist in Seoul, as part of Korea's liberation movement that taught women their rights. She moved to the United States in the late 1950s to study international and human relations at New York University. Focusing her studies on women and cultural change, she also started teaching classes for wives of foreign diplomats, to help them handle problems of cultural transition to the United States. By the 1960s, Lyu-Volckhausen and some friends had organized a Korean immigrant outreach center at the YWCA in Queens, New York. Since that time, the

YWCA program has grown to offer sewing classes, after-school recreation for children, counseling for battered women, and discussion groups on women's roles in American and Korean cultures.

Grace Lyu-Volckhausen has represented her community on the New York City Commission on the Status of Women, on the Mayor's Ethnic Council, and on Governor Mario Cuomo's Garment Advisory Council. She remains a chair of her YWCA youth committee and also works with a New York mortgage agency to provide affordable housing for minorities.

Grace Lyu-Volckhausen

Literature

Author Younghill Kang (1903–1972) was born in northern Korea and moved to the United States at age 18. He studied literature at Harvard University, then held a variety of jobs. He taught comparative literature at New York University and worked for the Encyclopaedia Britannica and the Metropolitan Museum of Art in New York City. He also served as a language consultant for the U.S. government during World War II. Kang is best known, however, for his books *The Grass Roof* (1931), which describes his life in Korea, and *East Goes West* (1937), which chronicles his search for identity as an Asian in America. In 1933, when Kang won a Guggenheim fellowship, he became the first Asian American to receive this award.

Another well-known writer of Korean descent is Richard E. Kim, born in Hamhung City, Korea, in 1932. Kim attended Middlebury College from 1955 to 1959 and later earned three masters degrees. He then began his career as an instructor in English at Long Beach State College, Long Beach, California, where he taught from 1963 to 1964. Later he became an assistant professor of English at the University of Massachusetts, Amherst. Before coming to the United States, Kim served in the Republic of Korea Army, as a first lieutenant. His war experiences became the subjects of his famous writings. His novel *The Martyred* (1964), an examination of human suffering and the human race's relationship to God during wartime, has been compared to the writings of the famous French novelist and playwright Albert Camus. In fact, Kim dedicated *The Martyred* to Camus because, Kim said, the French writer's "insights . . . overcame for me the nihilism of the trenches and bunkers of Korea." Richard Kim also wrote *The Innocent* (1968), and *Lost Names* (1970), a work of nonfiction.

Younghill Kang

Art

Now principally known as a video artist, Nam June Paik gained a worldwide reputation as a composer of electronic music and a producer of avant-garde "action concerts." Paik's theatrical performances of the 1960s featured such elements as musicians smashing a piano, or Paik himself running from the stage to pour shampoo over the heads of composers in the audience. Paik's more recent video work challenges viewers with comments on television as an artistic medium, television technology, and the role of television in society. His video work has been the focus of several major retrospectives around the world.

Paik was born in Seoul, Korea, in 1932. He was educated at the University of Tokyo from 1952 to 1956, where he earned a degree in aesthetics, but also studied Western music. He then studied music, art history, and philosophy in Germany between 1956 and 1958. It was while Paik was in Germany that he met American composer John Cage, who inspired Paik's interest in American electronic music. From 1958 to 1961, Paik worked in an electronic music studio for Radio Cologne, in Cologne, West Germany. He then returned to the United States and worked briefly as artist-in-residence for WGBH-TV in Boston and WNET-TV in New York.

Video artist and composer Nam June Paik, born in Seoul, now lives and works in New York City.

Paik's work has been exhibited in several cities in Germany, as well as at the Museum of Modern Art, the Whitney Museum, and The Kitchen in New York City, the Metropolitan Art Museum in Tokyo, and the Museum of Contemporary Art in Chicago. Some of his well-known video installations are *TV Buddha* (1974), in which a Buddha figurine reflects on its own image on a television screen, and *Video Fish* (1975), which displays tanks of live tropical fish amid televisions playing videotapes of fish. Nam June Paik also produced a simultaneous live broadcast from San Francisco, New York, and Paris of a program featuring numerous performing artists. The program, called *Good Morning, Mr. Orwell*, was a tribute to George Orwell, author of the book *1984*. It was broadcast on New Year's Day of 1984.

Music

Violinist Chouhei Min of the Minnesota Orchestra was associate concertmaster from 1976 to 1990. Born in Seoul, Min began to study violin at the age of five. The young musician was only nine years old when

Chouhei Min

she made her debut with the Seoul Philharmonic Orchestra. In 1965 she came to the United States to study at the Boston Conservatory of Music and the Hartt College of Music in Hartford, Connecticut. Before joining the Minnesota Orchestra, Chouhei Min was associate concertmaster of the Dallas Symphony Orchestra.

Earl Kim is a California-born composer of Korean heritage. He is best known for his musical settings of texts by Irish playwright and novelist Samuel Beckett. In 1979, Kim also wrote a violin concerto for violinist Itzhak Perlman. And Kim's *Where Grief Slumbers*, which sets works by French poets Rimbaud and Apollinaire to music, was performed by the American Composers Orchestra at Carnegie Hall in 1988.

Pianist and conductor Myung-whun Chung was just nine years old when he moved to Seattle, Washington, from Seoul, South Korea. His parents had obtained a visa to open a Korean restaurant at the 1962 Seattle World's Fair. Later that year, the young pianist made his American debut with the Seattle Symphony. Several years later, Chung moved to New York City to continue his studies. He enrolled at the Mannes College of Music in Manhattan, where he majored in conducting. In 1974, at the age of 21, Chung won second prize in the prestigious Tchaikovsky Piano Competition. That same year he gave a command performance for the South Korean president, Park Chung-hee, a Carnegie Hall solo recital, and a performance with the Philadelphia Orchestra.

Chung continued to study conducting at the Juilliard School. In 1975 he was named director of the Youth Symphony Orchestra of New York as well as music director and conductor of Juilliard's precollege orchestra. He toured as a pianist with two of his sisters—Myung-wha, a cellist, and Kyung-wha, a violinist—in a series of concerts sponsored by the American-Korean Cultural Association. After his graduation from Juilliard, Chung became the first assistant conductor of the Los Angeles Symphony Orchestra, a position he kept for three years. In 1981

Myung-whun Chun

he worked as guest conductor with the Berlin Philharmonic and the London Symphony Orchestra. In 1984 he was named director of the Saarland Radio Orchestra in West Germany and chief guest conductor of the Teatro Comunale, an opera house in Florence, Italy. He then went to Paris, where, in 1989, he was named music director of the Bastille Opera.

Entertainment

Character actor Philip Ahn (1919–1978), the eldest son of Korean diplomat and nationalist leader An Ch'ang-ho, was well known to American audiences for his appearances in many motion pictures and television programs. His acting career spanned more than 30 years. He had supporting roles in the popular films *The General Died at Dawn* (1936), *Thank You*

Mr. Moto (1937), and *Love Is a Many Splendored Thing* (1955). He was best known, however, for playing Chinese and Japanese villains in war films during the 1940s and 1950s. Among these were *Back to Bataan* (1945), *Halls of Montezuma* (1952), and *Battle Hymn* (1956). Then, in the 1970s, Ahn attracted a wide following in his role as a kung-fu master in the popular television series "Kung-Fu," which starred David Carradine. Ahn once remarked that while he had played hundreds of Asian roles, he was called upon to portray a Korean only once.

Philip Ahn

Randall Duk Kim is an exceptional actor who managed to escape ethnic stereotyping in the classical theater. Born in Hawaii to a Korean father and a Chinese mother, Kim has made a career playing Shakespearean roles and has gained a national reputation as one of the United States' most skilled interpreters of Shakespeare. He has played Prospero for the Indiana Repertory Company, Puck for the Yale Repertory Theatre, Richard III at San Francisco's American Conservatory Theater, and Pericles in The New York Shakespeare Festival in Central Park. In 1978 Kim joined one of the nation's outstanding repertory companies, the Guthrie Theater in Minneapolis, Minnesota. Kim does not wear makeup to try to change his facial features. His goal with each new play is to let the character take over his persona, so that the audience is not aware of an Asian actor, or of any actor, in the role. During his first season with the Guthrie, the versatile performer starred in *Hamlet*, played the part of an 80-year-old Norwegian man in Henrik Ibsen's *The Pretenders*, and portrayed a young Polish Jew in Isaac Bashevis Singer's *Teibele and Her Demon*.

In 1980 Randy Kim cofounded the American Players Theater in Spring Green, Wisconsin. In the founding production of the theater, Kim appeared as Walt Whitman in a one-person show. Kim remains active as an actor and artistic director of the American Players Theater, which explores classical dramatic literature, mainly Shakespeare.

Randall Duk Kim

Following Opening Day ceremonies at the 1988 Summer Olympic Games, Koreans cheered their fighters in the first athletic event: tae kwon do. The Korean martial art was an Olympic demonstration sport for the first time.

Sports

When Seoul, South Korea, hosted the 1988 Olympic Games, viewers all over the world became familiar with the Korean martial art of tae kwon do, which was featured in the Olympics that year as a demonstration sport. Since then, tae kwon do has increased in popularity throughout the United States, among Asian and non-Asian Americans alike. Nearly every major city has tae kwon do instructional schools.

Jim Paek, a hockey player who was born in Seoul, is one of very few Korean Americans to become involved in Western professional sports. He joined the Pittsburgh Penguins in the 1990–1991 season, and in the off-season he coached a Korean-Canadian hockey team that traveled to Korea for a tournament there.

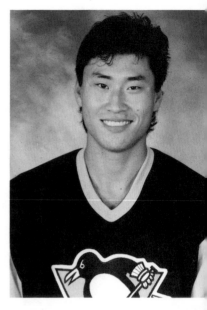

Jim Paek

Dr. Sammy Lee, born in Fresno, California, in 1920, was awarded the gold medal for 10-meter platform diving in the 1948 Olympic Games in London. Four years later, at the Olympic Games in Helsinki, Finland, he again won the gold medal for 10-meter platform diving, as well as the bronze medal in 3-meter springboard diving. Lee was already a doctor by this time. He received his M.D. in 1947 from the University of Southern California School of Medicine, where he took up diving as a student. He then served as a doctor in Korea from 1943 to 1955, as a part of the U.S. Army Medical Corps.

In 1953, while in Seoul with his Army unit, Lee received the news that he had won the James E. Sullivan Memorial Trophy, an award given to the outstanding American athlete of the year by the Amateur Athletic Union. In 1968 he was named to the International Swimming Hall of Fame. Dr. Lee served as a member of the President's Council on Physical Fitness and Sports from 1971 to 1980, and he coached the U.S. diving team for the 1960 and 1964 Olympic Games. He was also Greg Louganis's coach for the 1976 Montreal Olympics, where Louganis won a silver medal for the United States in platform diving.

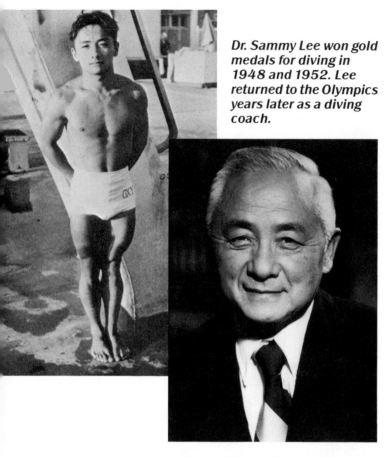

Dr. Sammy Lee won gold medals for diving in 1948 and 1952. Lee returned to the Olympics years later as a diving coach.

Dr. Lee was named the Outstanding American of Korean Ancestry by the American Korean Society in 1967 and the Outstanding American of Korean Ancestry by the League of Korean Americans in 1986. After retiring from an active career in sports, Dr. Lee owned a private medical practice in Orange, California, for many years. He specialized in otology, the branch of medicine that deals with diseases and disorders of the ear.

Throughout their history, Korean Americans have met with hardship. They have also succeeded— through hard work and determination, and through the strength of their own communities. As their numbers increase, Korean Americans continue to influence life and culture in the United States.

INDEX

ACKNOWLEDGMENTS The photographs in this book are reproduced through the courtesy of: p. 2, Hawaii State Archives; p. 6, The Lee Family, Wilmette, Illinois; p. 9, Korean Overseas Information Service; p. 10, The Bettman Archive; pp. 11, 28, The U.S. Information Agency, National Archives; p. 12, The Philip Jaisohn Memorial Foundation, Philadelphia, PA; p. 13, Library of Congress; p. 14, Independent Picture Service; p. 15, U.S. Army; pp. 17, 20, American Embassy, San Francisco; p. 18 (top and bottom), Reuters/Bettman Newsphotos; pp. 21, 22, 24, 26, 63, Bishop Museum; pp. 23, 25, Ray Jerome Baker/Bishop Museum; p. 27, City Photo/Bishop Museum; p. 29, Lucille H. Sukalo; pp. 31, 34-35, 41, 42, Visual Communications Archives; pp. 32, 43, 45, 46, 50, 58, 64, *Korea-Times,* Los Angeles; pp. 33, 38, 39, 52, UPI/Bettman; p. 36, National Archives; p. 52, Office of Judge Herbert Y. C. Choy; pp. 48-49, Hyundai Motor America; p. 51, Grace Lyu-Volckhausen; p. 53, J. M. Cockerill/Carl Solway Gallery; p. 54, Minnesota Orchestra; p. 56, Viviane Purdom/Opera de Paris Bastille; p. 57 (top), Lew Deuser Agency; p. 57 (bottom), The Guthrie Theater; p. 59, The Pittsburgh Penguins; p. 60 (top), International Swimming Hall of Fame; p. 60 (bottom), Dr. Sammy Lee.

Front and back cover photographs, Okmi Kim/*Komerican.*

A Korean-American Boy Scout troop in Honolulu, 1919

Groups featured in Lerner's In America series:

AMERICAN INDIANS   KOREANS
DANES   LEBANESE
FILIPINOS   MEXICANS
FRENCH   NORWEGIANS
GREEKS   PUERTO RICANS
ITALIANS   SCOTS &
JAPANESE   SCOTCH-IRISH
JEWS   VIETNAMESE

 Lerner Publications Company
241 First Avenue North • Minneapolis, Minnesota 55401